THE NERVOUS SYSTEM

Words in *italic* in the main
text (*or in* Roman *type in the
captions*) are explained in the
Index and glossary at the end
of the book.

A Cherrytree Book

Adapted by A S Publishing
from *EL SISTEMA NERVIOSO*
NUESTRO PROCESSO DE DATOS
by Núria Roca and Marta Serrano
illustrated by Antonio Muñoz Tenllado
designed by Rosa Mª Moreno
produced by Rafael Marfil
© Parramón Ediciones, S.A. 1995

This edition published 1996
by Cherrytree Press Ltd
a subsidiary of
The Chivers Company Ltd
Windsor Bridge Road
Bath, Avon BA2 3AX

British Library Cataloguing in Publication Data

The nervous system. – (Invisible world)
    1. Nervous system – Juvenile literature 2. Neuroanatomy –
    Juvenile literature
    I. Halton, Frances
    611.8

ISBN 0-7451-5281-3

Typeset by Dorchester Typesetting, Group Ltd. Dorset
Printed in Spain

INVISIBLE WORLD

THE NERVOUS SYSTEM

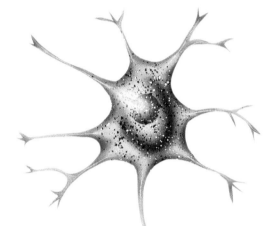

Edited by
Frances Halton

CHERRYTREE BOOKS

Our information system

Can you hear anything? Are you too hot or too cold? What can you see? All the time, our bodies are taking in information about the world around us – our *external environment*. This information is picked up by special cells called sense *receptors*. Inside our bodies, more receptors are monitoring what is going on inside us – our *internal environment*. They check whether our *muscles* are stretched, the amount of *oxygen* and *carbon dioxide* in our blood and so on.

We need this information for our survival. To stay healthy and avoid danger, we have to be aware of what is going on around us, and our bodies have to work efficiently. An immensely complicated system, called the nervous system, takes in information, processes it and prompts us to take what actions are necessary.

The receptors send messages along *sensory nerves* to the *spinal cord* and the *brain*, where the information is processed. Then messages are sent down *motor nerves* to muscles and organs which can carry out any necessary actions. Sometimes these actions are conscious decisions, such as turning on a heater when we feel cold. Sometimes they happen without any conscious decision; when we are very cold we shiver, which is one of the body's ways of warming us up. Very often we do not even notice what our bodies are doing; did you know that the tiny *blood vessels* near the skin get thinner when you are cold? This is another of the body's ways of stopping our temperature from dropping dangerously low.

The nervous system has two main divisions. The *peripheral nervous system* is responsible for collecting all the information, and delivering instructions to muscles and other organs. The *central nervous system*, made up of the spinal cord and the brain, is where the information is received and interpreted and where responses to it are initiated. It is so immensely complicated that we still have a great deal to learn about the way it works.

The most complicated part of all is the brain. It processes most of the sensory information, controlling all our *conscious actions* and almost all our *unconscious actions*, including breathing, circulation and *digestion*. It is also where our *higher mental functions* take place. These include conscious thought, perception, reasoning, learning, memory, language and imagination.

When your body receives a stimulus from its environment, for instance a drop in temperature, you feel a sensation – in this case cold. Your body responds in a number of ways. The tiny hairs on your skin stand on end and trap a layer of warm air next to the skin. The blood vessels close to the skin contract, so that the blood loses less heat. You shiver, which helps raise your body's temperature. These are all involuntary, unconscious reactions. Voluntary, conscious actions to warm you up might include moving around, putting on more clothes and turning on a heater.

▼

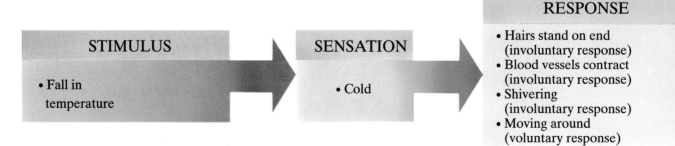

STIMULUS
- Fall in temperature

SENSATION
- Cold

RESPONSE
- Hairs stand on end (involuntary response)
- Blood vessels contract (involuntary response)
- Shivering (involuntary response)
- Moving around (voluntary response)

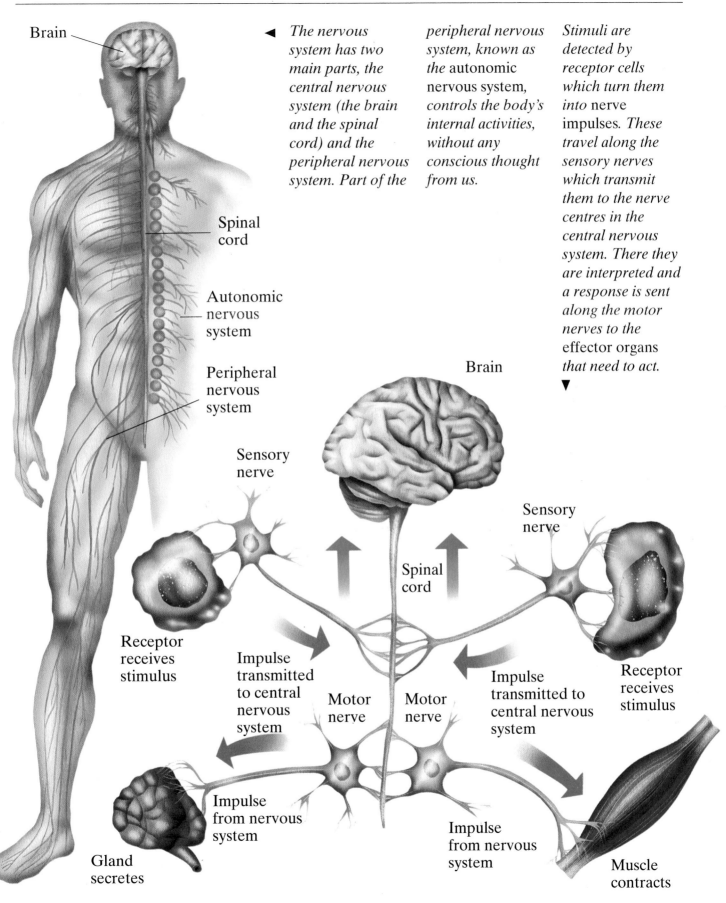

Brain

Spinal cord

Autonomic nervous system

Peripheral nervous system

The nervous system has two main parts, the central nervous system (the brain and the spinal cord) and the peripheral nervous system. Part of the peripheral nervous system, known as the autonomic nervous system, controls the body's internal activities, without any conscious thought from us.

Stimuli are detected by receptor cells which turn them into nerve impulses. These travel along the sensory nerves which transmit them to the nerve centres in the central nervous system. There they are interpreted and a response is sent along the motor nerves to the effector organs that need to act.

Brain

Sensory nerve

Sensory nerve

Spinal cord

Receptor receives stimulus

Receptor receives stimulus

Impulse transmitted to central nervous system

Impulse transmitted to central nervous system

Motor nerve

Motor nerve

Impulse from nervous system

Impulse from nervous system

Gland secretes

Muscle contracts

The neurons

The nervous system is made up of millions of interconnected nerve cells called *neurons*. These are specialized cells that send signals called nerve impulses. They pass them on to other neurons, or to muscles and *glands*. Unlike other cells in the body, neurons cannot be replaced when they die or are damaged.

A typical neuron is made up of the cell body containing the *nucleus*, and two types of extension: *dendrites* and *axons*. They are known as nerve fibres. The dendrites carry *nerve impulses* to the cell body. They are usually short, with a wide base and treelike branches. Most neurons have several dendrites and just one axon. This carries nerve impulses from the cell body to other neurons or other parts of the body.

An axon usually has a narrower base than a dendrite, and a thin stem which may be a metre long. At the end it divides into tiny branches, each ending in a minute knob, or terminal. Axons are grouped together in bundles known as nerves.

Some axons are protected by a sheath of a white, fatty substance called *myelin*. In the central nervous system this is made by supporting cells called *glial cells*. In the peripheral nervous system myelin is formed by Schwann cells. The myelin sheath has occasional gaps in it, called *nodes of Ranvier*. The myelin is white, while the cell bodies are grey. As a result, parts of the nervous system that are largely made up of cell bodies and unsheathed axons are greyish in colour, and known as *grey matter*. Areas made up mostly of axons with their myelin sheaths are known as *white matter*.

Neurons are connected to one another in a complex network of pathways, along which information travels from one part of the body to another.

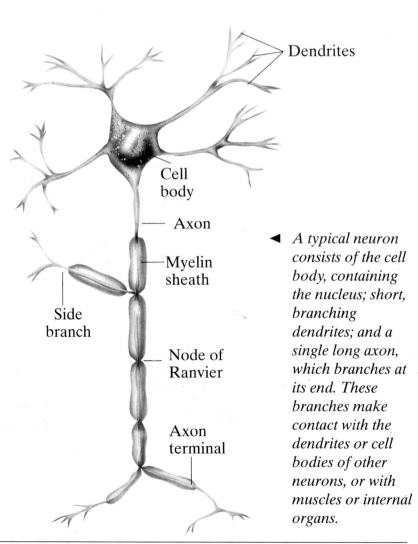

Dendrites

Cell body

Axon

Myelin sheath

Side branch

Node of Ranvier

Axon terminal

◀ *A typical neuron consists of the cell body, containing the nucleus; short, branching dendrites; and a single long axon, which branches at its end. These branches make contact with the dendrites or cell bodies of other neurons, or with muscles or internal organs.*

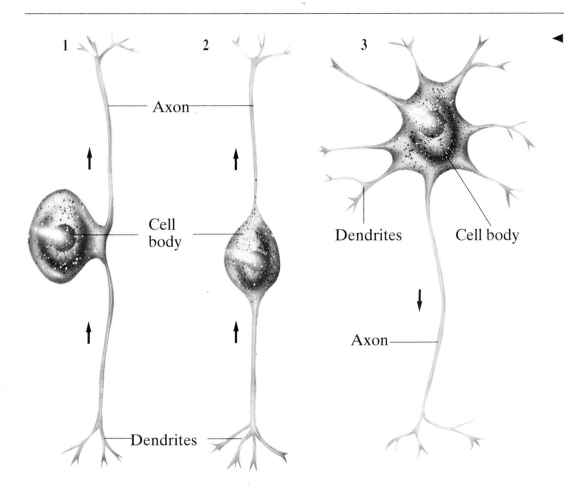

1   2   3

Axon

Cell body

Dendrites   Cell body

Axon

Dendrites

◀ Neurons can be classified by their length and shape. Unipolar neurons (**1**) have a single projection from the cell body, which divides into two branches, one of which sends impulses to the cell body, the other from it. Bipolar neurons (**2**) have two separate projections, a dendron and an axon leaving from opposite sides. Most common are multipolar neurons (**3**), which have a number of dendrites and a single axon.

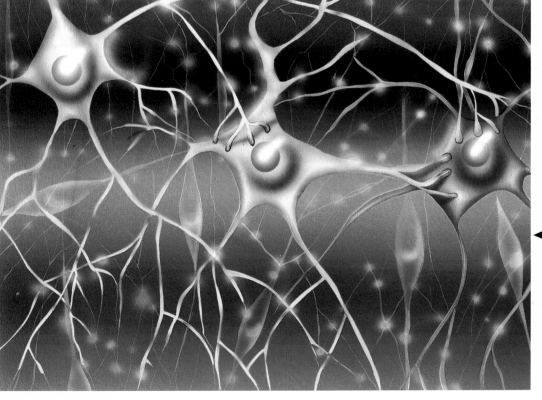

◀ Neurons interconnect with one another to form networks along which nerve impulses travel. They are like printed circuits on a computer chip.

Nerve impulses

Neurons pass information from one part of the body to another by means of nerve impulses. At one time people thought these were like the electrical impulses sent down a wire, but we now know that they work by an electrochemical process, a mixture of electricity and chemistry. This is based on the relative number of electrically positive and negative particles called *ions* inside and outside the cell membrane.

When a neuron is at rest, there are more positively charged particles or *ions* outside than inside its membrane, and more negative ions inside than outside. The cell membrane stops the ions crossing to even the balance, so there is an electrical charge between the outside and inside of the nerve cell which is called the *resting potential.*

A nerve impulse begins when some stimulus makes tiny gaps open in part of the neuron's membrane. Immediately, positive ions move in, and negative ions move out. The charge between the inside and the outside of this area of the cell's membrane is reversed. This process is called *depolarization*, and the inverted charge is called the *action potential.*

An action potential in one part of the cell opens gaps farther down the membrane, and again the ions move across. In this way, the impulse travels along the axon. As soon as it has passed, the positive ions are pushed out of the cell and the original charge – the resting potential – comes back. The cell is ready for the next impulse.

All this happens extremely quickly, in hundredths of a second, and the larger the diameter of the neuron, the faster this impulse travels. The impulse travels more rapidly along axons covered by a myelin sheath, because the exchange of ions only takes place in the nodes of Ranvier, and not along the whole length of the membrane. This type of transmission is called saltatory (jumping) conduction.

Many different stimuli can set off an action potential, from an injury such as a pinprick to changes in the environment such as heat or cold, to sounds or smells.

When an axon is covered by a myelin sheath (top), ions cannot freely enter and exit, so the reversal of the charge along its membrane takes place only at the nodes of Ranvier in a series of jumps. The nerve impulse travels much faster along these axons than along those without a sheath (bottom), where the reversals happen much more frequently. ▼

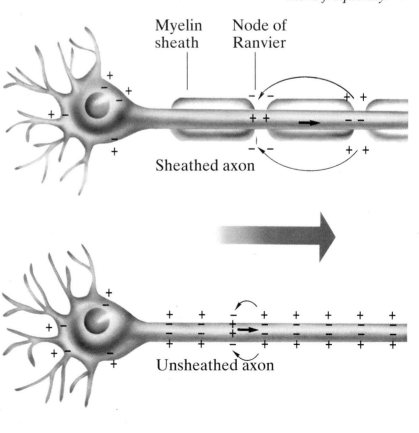

Myelin sheath

Node of Ranvier

Sheathed axon

Unsheathed axon

The myelin sheath ▶ *(1) around the axon (2) is formed by extensions of the glial cells (3) that support the neurons. Only the nodes of Ranvier (4) are left uncovered.*

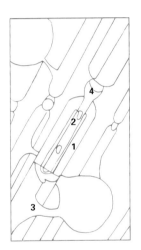

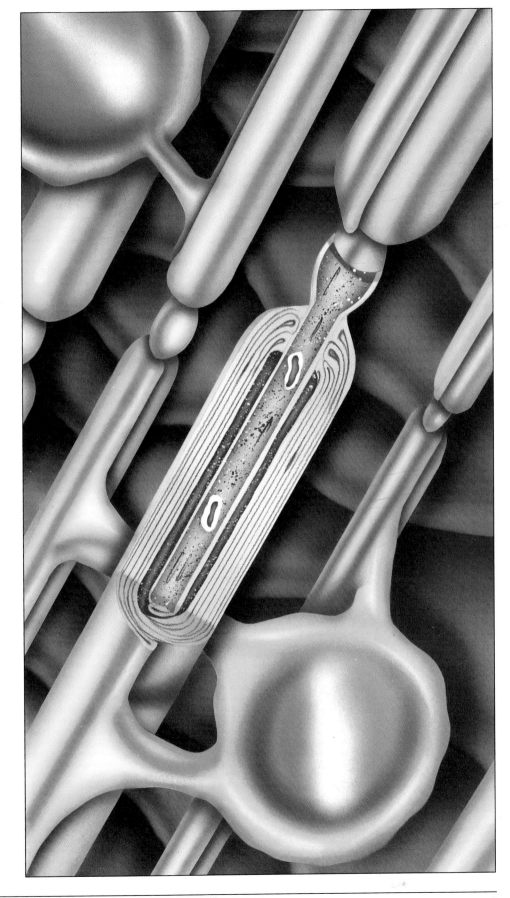

From neuron to neuron

Nerve impulses pass from one neuron to another, but the neurons do not touch each other. There is a slight gap between them called a *synapse*. The impulse from the end of an axon is generally picked up by the dendrites of the next neuron, or it may pass directly to the cell body.

Sometimes the impulse crosses the synapse with a 'spark' of electricity, but more usually it happens through a chemical process.

This chemical transmission is carried out through *neurotransmitters*. These are chemicals produced by the neurons that cause pores to open in the neuron's membrane.

Neurotransmitters are stored in *vesicles* in the terminals at the ends of an axon. When a nerve impulse arrives at the terminal, the vesicles empty their neurotransmitters into the synapse. They cross to the membrane of the next neuron, where they react with special receptor sites. This opens tiny gaps in the membrane and so sets off an action potential which this second neuron transmits down its own axon. The neurotransmitters are quickly taken up by the vesicles in the axon terminals again, or are destroyed by other chemicals.

*When an impulse arrives at the terminal of an axon (**1**), neurotransmitters (**2**) are released by the vesicles (**3**). The* ▼

*neurotransmitters lock on to receptors on the next neuron (**4**) that allow pores to open in the membrane and ions to cross.*

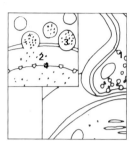

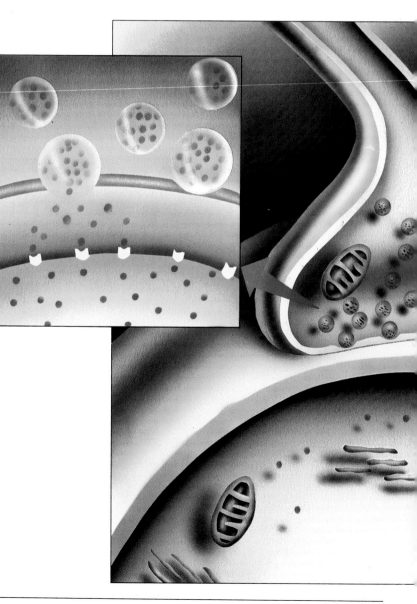

*Different types of neurotransmitter can be released into the synapse, making the potential excitatory (**1**) or inhibitory (**2**), the former passing on the impulse, the latter preventing its passage. Under a microscope, excitatory vesicles appear round, inhibitory ones lengthened.*

▼

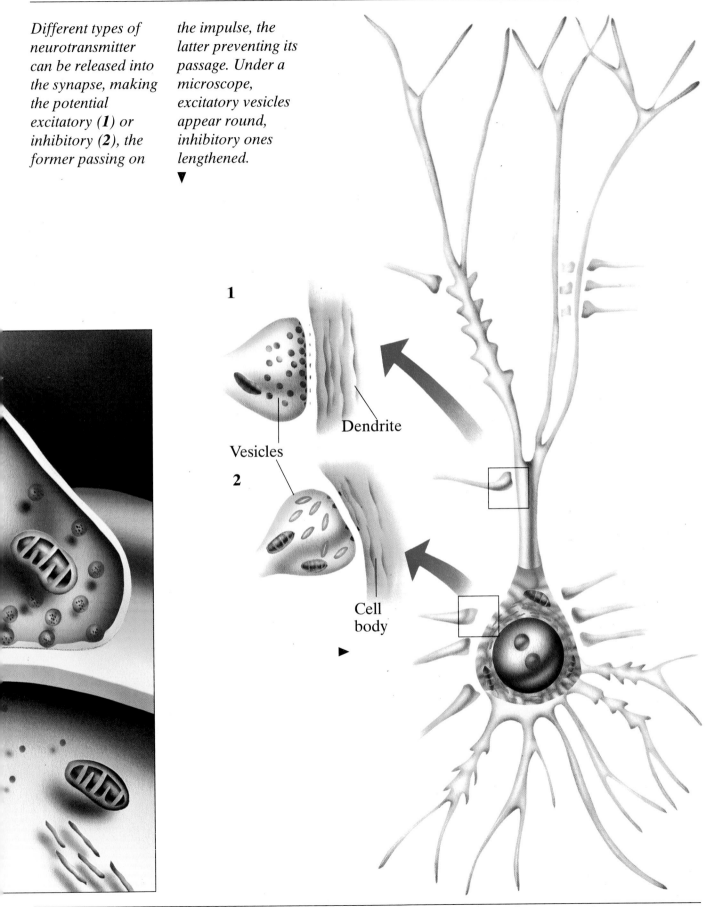

1

Vesicles

Dendrite

2

Cell body

▶

The central nervous system

The central nervous system, consisting of the brain and the spinal cord, regulates the working of all the different parts of the body. The brain receives and interprets information from receptors all over the body, decides what action if any should be taken, and sends off instructions to carry out the action. The brain is also in charge of our higher mental functions.

The vital parts of the central nervous system are well protected. The brain is safely enclosed inside the bones of the skull, and the spinal cord runs through the channel in the centre of the *vertebrae* of the *spinal column*. Both the brain and the spinal cord are surrounded by membranes called *meninges* which support and protect them.

The meninges are made up of three layers. The tough, fibrous outer layer is called the *dura mater*. The part surrounding the brain is attached to the bones of the skull. Next comes the weblike *arachnoid layer*, and finally the delicate *pia mater*. This is directly in contact with the surface of the brain and the spinal cord, and contains blood vessels to nourish the neurons.

Between the meninges and in the spaces in and around the brain and spinal cord is a watery liquid called *cerebrospinal fluid*. This contains substances that nourish the neurons, and *white cells* that fight infections. The fluid also acts as a shock-absorber. If you bang your head, it cushions the brain and prevents it banging against the skull bones.

The brain and the spinal cord are made up of grey and white matter. In the brain grey matter forms the outer, visible layer, while in the spinal cord the grey matter is in the centre, surrounded by white matter.

The central nervous system is protected by membranes called meninges. These have three layers. The outer layer (1) is called the dura mater and is the hardest. It lies next to the bones of the skull (2) and the spine. Next comes the arachnoid layer (3). Between it and the delicate inner

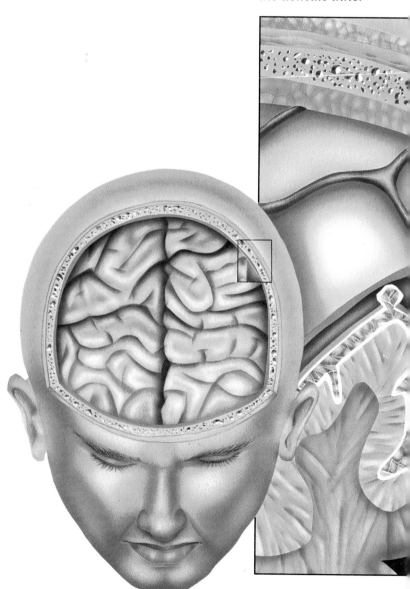

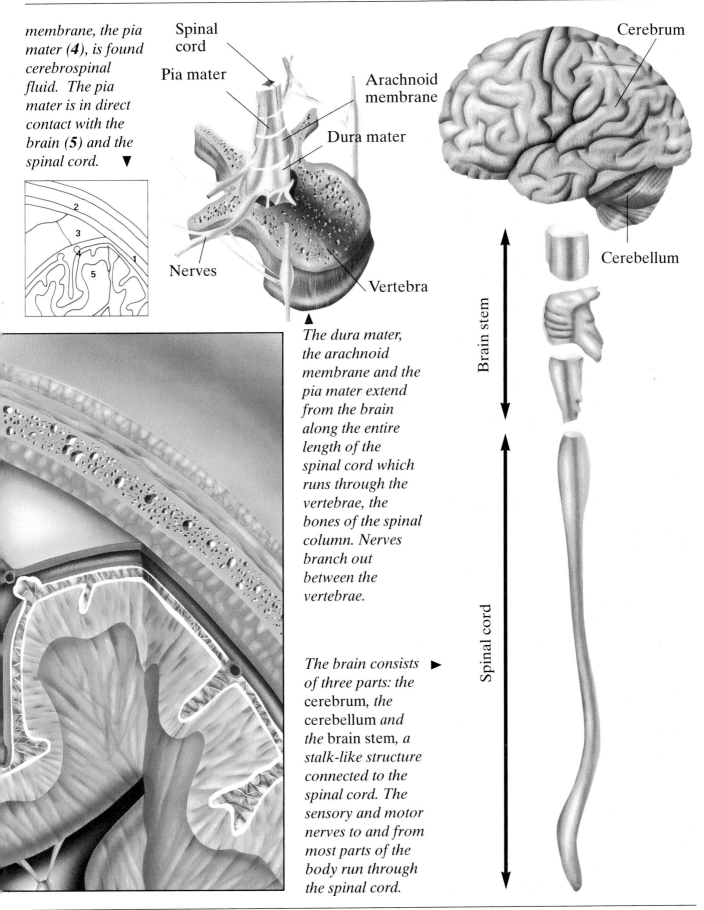

membrane, the pia mater (4), is found cerebrospinal fluid. The pia mater is in direct contact with the brain (5) and the spinal cord. ▼

Spinal cord

Pia mater

Arachnoid membrane

Dura mater

Cerebrum

Cerebellum

Nerves

Vertebra

Brain stem

Spinal cord

▲ *The dura mater, the arachnoid membrane and the pia mater extend from the brain along the entire length of the spinal cord which runs through the vertebrae, the bones of the spinal column. Nerves branch out between the vertebrae.*

The brain consists ► *of three parts: the* cerebrum, *the* cerebellum *and the* brain stem, *a stalk-like structure connected to the spinal cord. The sensory and motor nerves to and from most parts of the body run through the spinal cord.*

The brain

The brain is the headquarters of the central nervous system. It contains some 15,000 million neurons, each linked to other cells by thousands of nerve fibres. They make up an immensely complicated network of paths along which nerve signals can travel.

The largest and most obvious part of the brain – the cerebrum – is made up of two *cerebral hemispheres.* Their outer surface, the *cerebral cortex,* is a layer of grey matter about two millimetres thick, which is deeply wrinkled and folded to fit into the skull. Each hemisphere is made up of four main lobes, and the two hemispheres are connected to each other by a band of nerve fibres called the *corpus callosum.*

All the conscious sensations from our sense receptors are sent to the cells of the cerebral cortex, where they are interpreted and responded to. Different areas of the cortex deal with the different senses and with our higher functions.

Below the cerebral cortex is a layer of white matter, nerve fibres that connect parts of the cortex and link it with other parts of the brain and spinal cord. Under this, at the top of the brain stem, lies the *thalamus,* which sorts out sensory messages and sends them to the appropriate part of the cortex. Nearby is the *hypothalamus.* This links the nervous system with the *endocrine glands,* and regulates the autonomic nervous system. It is involved in appetite and thirst, temperature, changes in blood pressure and sleep.

Below the cerebral hemispheres lies the deeply grooved mass of grey matter called the cerebellum. It is involved in co-ordinating balance and the activity of our muscles, so that we can move around smoothly. It receives information from different parts of the body and from the cerebral cortex.

The lowest part of the brain is called the brain stem. It includes the *pons,* the *medulla oblongata* and the *reticular formation.* They help to control the body's vital functions such as breathing, heartbeat, blood pressure and consciousness.

As they pass through the medulla, sensory nerves arriving from the right side of the body cross over to go to the left side of the brain, and nerves from the left side of the body cross to the right side of the brain. This means that all the information from your right side is dealt with in the left hemisphere, and an injury to that part of your brain will affect the right side of your body.

Ridges called ▶
gyri and fissures called sulci *divide each hemisphere of the brain into four main lobes, named after the skull bones that cover them.*

The greater part of ▶
the brain is made up of two cerebral hemispheres, joined by the corpus callosum. Beneath this lies the cerebellum, which is important in co-ordinating our movements, and the brain stem which includes the pons, the medulla oblongata and the reticular formation.

Frontal
lobe

Temporal
lobe

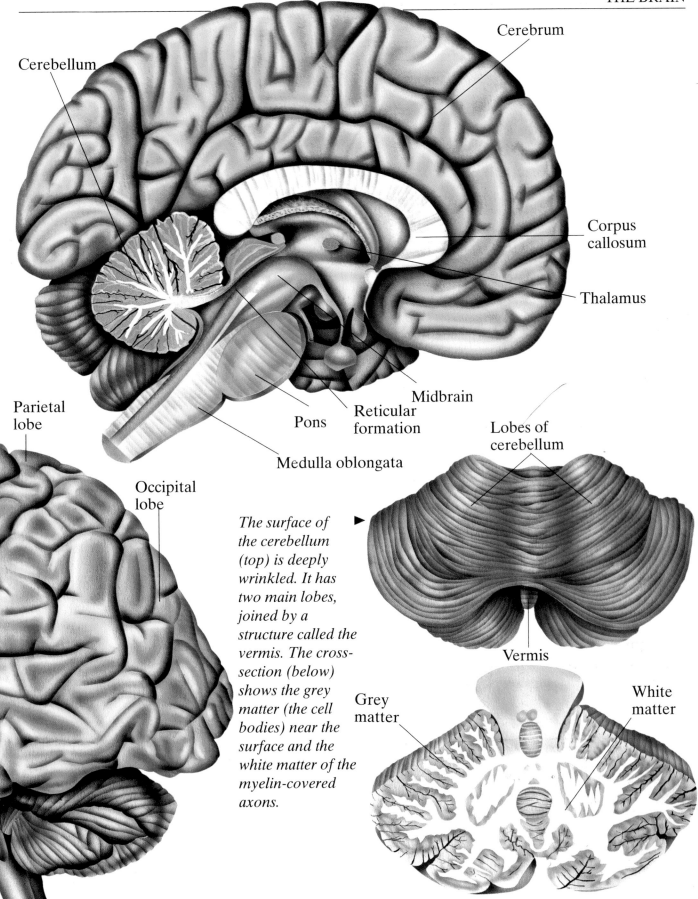

Cerebellum

Cerebrum

Corpus callosum

Thalamus

Midbrain

Pons

Reticular formation

Medulla oblongata

Parietal lobe

Occipital lobe

Lobes of cerebellum

Vermis

Grey matter

White matter

The surface of the cerebellum (top) is deeply wrinkled. It has two main lobes, joined by a structure called the vermis. The cross-section (below) shows the grey matter (the cell bodies) near the surface and the white matter of the myelin-covered axons.

The spinal cord

The spinal cord is a long, cylindrical structure that stretches down the back from the base of the brain to the bottom of the spine. It runs along a channel inside the vertebrae. In adults it is about 45 centimetres long.

The spinal cord is divided into 31 segments: the 8 cervical segments in the neck, 12 thoracic, or dorsal, segments behind the chest, 5 lumbar in the small of the back, 5 sacral and 1 coccygeal. These segments correspond with the bones that make up the spine. A pair of nerves (each a bundle of nerve fibres) emerges from each segment, through the spaces between the vertebrae. One of each pair goes to either side of the body.

The outer part of the spinal cord is made up of white matter, which consists of sensory and motor nerve axons taking nerve impulses to and from the brain. This surrounds a centre, or medulla, of grey matter. It is shaped like a butterfly, or H, the corners of which are called horns. The front (ventral) part contains motor neurons, and the rear (dorsal) part is made up of connector and sensory neurons.

The neurons in the spinal cord process impulses from the sensory nerves. Some are sent up to the brain to be interpreted and for decisions to be taken, and instructions sent back to the motor nerves. Other impulses are dealt with by the spinal cord's grey matter in *reflex responses*, which are so quick that we do not 'think' about them. Among these are reflexes that pro-

tect the body. For example, when you prick your finger a receptor cell in the skin receives the painful stimulus, which then travels along the sensory nerve to the spinal cord. There it is transmitted across the synapses to the motor neurons. They send nerve impulses to the muscles of the hand to jerk away from the object pricking it. There is no time for the stimulus to travel all the way to the brain before our bodies take action, although the information does travel to the brain as well, rather more slowly.

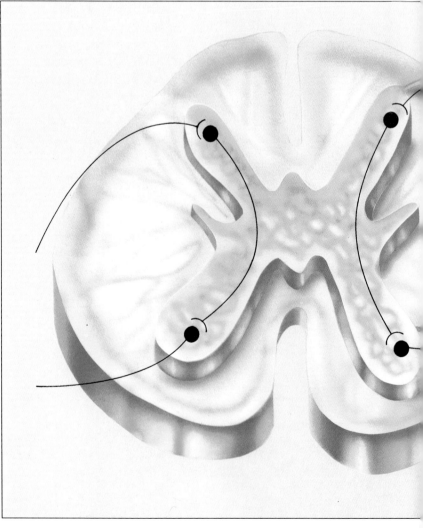

This cross-section ►
of the spinal cord
shows the white
matter on the
outside and the
grey matter in the
centre, shaped like
an H. It has two
ventral horns,
pointing towards
the front of the
body, and two
thinner dorsal
horns.

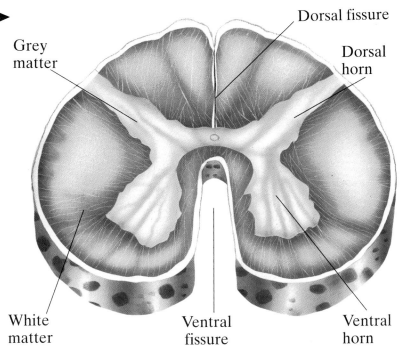

Grey
matter

Dorsal fissure

Dorsal
horn

White
matter

Ventral
fissure

Ventral
horn

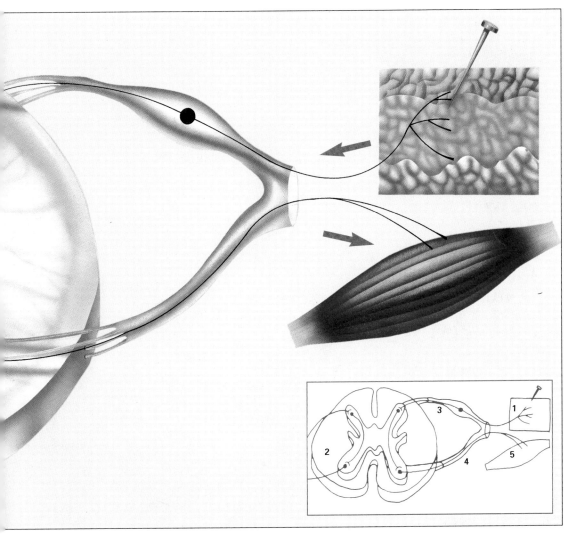

◄ *A painful stimulus*
(1) causes a reflex
action, an
automatic
response out of
our conscious
control. The
response to the
stimulus comes
directly from the
spinal cord (2),
without needing to
pass through the
brain. The impulse
from the receptor
travels through the
sensory nerve (3)
to the spinal cord
where it passes
across synapses to
the motor nerve
(4) which sends
commands to the
muscles (5). They
move instantly to
prevent further
harm to the body.

The nerves

The peripheral nervous system is made up of nerves, bundles of many individual nerve fibres wrapped in a fibrous sheath that protects and nourishes them. The nerves connect the central nervous system with all parts of the body.

The sensory nerve fibres of the peripheral nervous system take messages from the body's receptor cells to the central nervous system. Motor nerve fibres carry instructions for action back to the effector organs.

The peripheral nervous system has two divisions. The *somatic system* connects sense receptors with the central nervous system and the central nervous system with the muscles of the skeleton, through which we move. Except for reflex actions, the actions it controls are conscious ones.

The autonomic nervous system works without our conscious control. It regulates the functioning of our *internal organs*, glands and particular muscles, including those of the *heart* and the *digestive system*.

Twelve pairs of nerves lead directly to and from the brain. They are called *cranial nerves*. Almost all of them supply muscles and sense organs in the head and neck, but one pair goes down to the heart, the lungs and the *abdomen* and regulates mostly autonomic processes. Some cranial nerves consist solely of sensory nerve fibres, others solely of motor nerve fibres, and others of a mixture of the two.

Another 31 pairs of nerves go to and from the spinal cord. These are all mixed nerves. One of each pair leads to the right side of the body and the other to the left. As they move away from the spinal cord, they branch out into smaller and smaller nerves which lead to organs, muscles and skin.

In the skin, the sensory nerves end at receptors that are sensitive to touch, pain, pressure or temperature. Sense receptors are also found in the muscles and the internal organs, among them receptors that sense how far a muscle has been stretched, the state of the blood and the body's internal temperature. The branching ends of the motor nerves transmit the impulses that activate the effector organs.

Some cranial nerves are sensory, some motor and some mixed. There are 12 pairs, some with two or more branches:
1, 2 & 8 transmit messages about smell, sight and sound respectively. 3, 4 & 6 are made up of motor nerves responsible for some movements of the eye.
5 & 7 are mixed nerves, acting on the muscles of the face as well as

Each spinal nerve leaves the spinal cord in two branches, sensory nerve fibres from the back part, the dorsal root, and motor nerve fibres from the front part, the ventral root. They then join to form the nerve. ▼

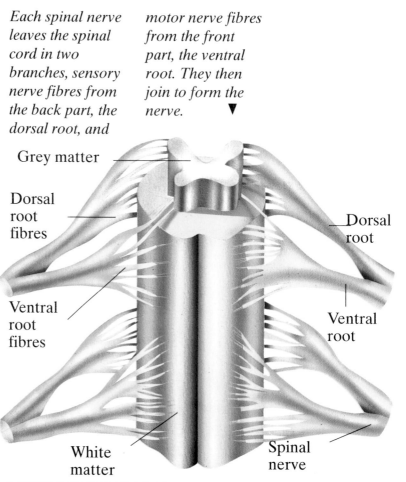

Grey matter

Dorsal root fibres

Ventral root fibres

White matter

Dorsal root

Ventral root

Spinal nerve

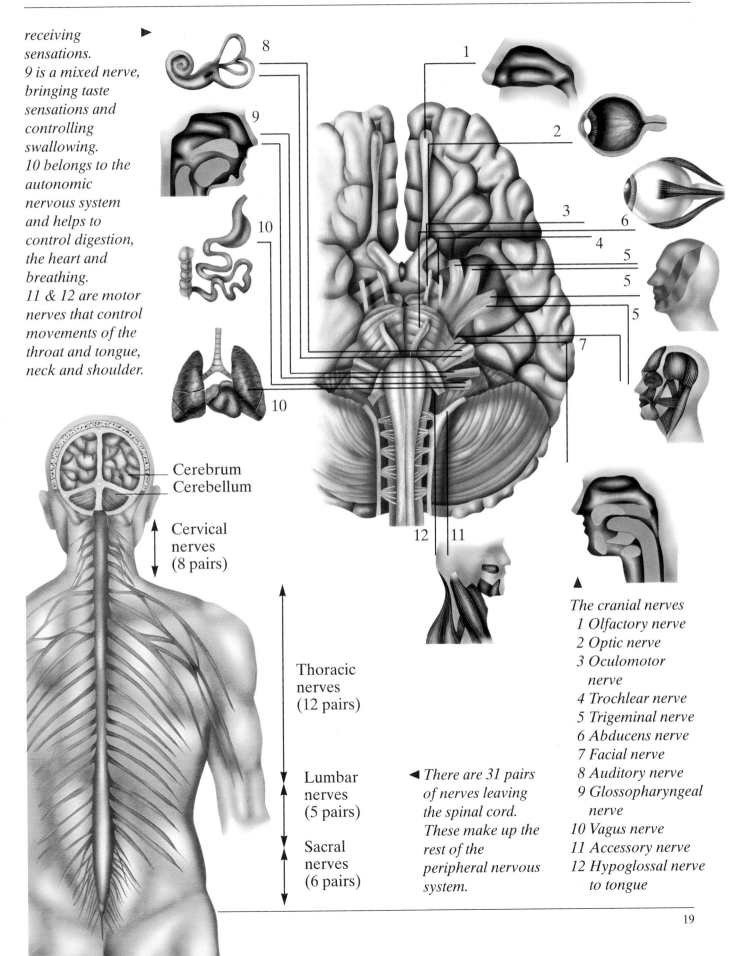

receiving sensations. 9 is a mixed nerve, bringing taste sensations and controlling swallowing. 10 belongs to the autonomic nervous system and helps to control digestion, the heart and breathing. 11 & 12 are motor nerves that control movements of the throat and tongue, neck and shoulder.

8

9

10

10

1

2

3

6

4

5

5

5

7

12   11

Cerebrum
Cerebellum

Cervical nerves (8 pairs)

Thoracic nerves (12 pairs)

Lumbar nerves (5 pairs)

Sacral nerves (6 pairs)

◄ *There are 31 pairs of nerves leaving the spinal cord. These make up the rest of the peripheral nervous system.*

▲
The cranial nerves
1 Olfactory nerve
2 Optic nerve
3 Oculomotor nerve
4 Trochlear nerve
5 Trigeminal nerve
6 Abducens nerve
7 Facial nerve
8 Auditory nerve
9 Glossopharyngeal nerve
10 Vagus nerve
11 Accessory nerve
12 Hypoglossal nerve to tongue

Sense receptors

All the time, our nerves are sending to the brain enormous amounts of information about our external environment and about our internal environment: whether we are tired or hungry, have aching muscles, a full bladder and so on. The sensory cells responsible for picking up this information are called receptors.

These sensory cells detect variations in the internal and external environments and turn them into nerve impulses. We are conscious of many sensations, but other receptors, particularly those concerned with the everyday functioning of digestion, breathing and so on, send impulses that are dealt with by the autonomic system, and we are not aware of them. When there is too much carbon dioxide in the blood, for example, receptors will notice and as a result of their information we will breathe faster to get rid of it.

The receptor cells for different senses are quite different from one another, and each reacts to one particular stimulus only. Some, like the touch receptors, are scattered all over the body; others are grouped together to form sensory organs such as the eyes. Those that detect changes in the environment, such as light or sound, are called exterior receptors. Those detecting changes within the body, such as muscular tension, are called proprioceptors.

The following types of receptor have been identified.

Mechanoreceptors detect mechanical stimuli. Those in the skin conduct the sensations of touch, pressure and pain. Others detect stretching of muscles and sound waves.

Thermoreceptors, also found in the skin, detect heat and cold. They can also detect pain.

Chemoreceptors detect chemical changes in their environment. They include olfactory receptors in the nose through which we smell, taste receptors that are sensitive to liquids and solids, and receptors that detect changes in the oxygen, carbon dioxide and acidity levels in the blood.

Photoreceptors in the eye are stimulated by light.

Statoreceptors in the semicircular canals of the ear give us information about the position of the body in relation to its surroundings. They provide our sense of balance.

Phonoreceptors in the organ of Corti in the inner ear detect sound.

There are also many *free nerve endings* in skin, muscles and our internal organs. These are not so specialized; they detect pain, and in some cases pressure and temperature.

Some of our receptors are able to adapt to stimuli. When you get dressed, the nerve endings in the skin notice the contact with your clothes at first, but after a time they get used to the feeling and cease to be stimulated, so that you no longer notice the touch of the cloth on your skin. The same happens when you get into a swimming pool; at first the water feels cold, but after a little while you do not feel it any more.

Touch, temperature ▶ and pain receptors are found all over the surface of the body, scattered unevenly. For example, we have many more touch receptors on our fingertips than on the backs of the fingers; the tips are much more sensitive.

The olfactory ▶ receptor cells that detect smells are found in the membrane lining the nose. They send nerve impulses to the olfactory lobe of the brain.

In the retina of the ▶ eye are two types of light receptor. Cone cells detect colour and fine detail; rod cells cannot detect colour but are so sensitive to light that they enable us to see even when it is dim. There are about 125 million rods and only 7 million cones.

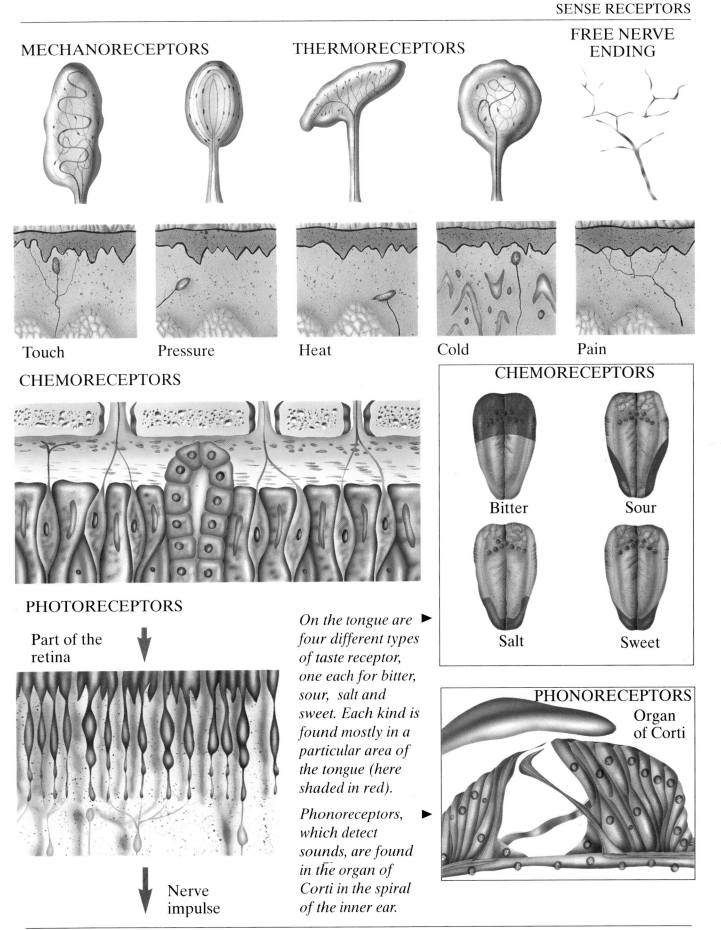

MECHANORECEPTORS

THERMORECEPTORS

FREE NERVE ENDING

Touch   Pressure   Heat   Cold   Pain

CHEMORECEPTORS

CHEMORECEPTORS

Bitter   Sour

Salt   Sweet

PHOTORECEPTORS

Part of the retina

Nerve impulse

On the tongue are ▶ four different types of taste receptor, one each for bitter, sour, salt and sweet. Each kind is found mostly in a particular area of the tongue (here shaded in red).

Phonoreceptors, ▶ which detect sounds, are found in the organ of Corti in the spiral of the inner ear.

PHONORECEPTORS

Organ of Corti

Making sense

We still have a great deal to learn about how the brain works, but we do know that many of its functions are carried out by special areas of the cerebral cortex, the wrinkled layer of grey matter covering the cerebral hemispheres.

One of the vital functions of the brain is to receive and interpret sensations from all over the body, and to send out responses to them. Each part of the body is connected by its sensory nerves to a particular part of the cerebral cortex where information from its sense receptors is interpreted. Our responses are initiated in the motor areas of the cortex, which again has areas dedicated to different parts of the body.

These areas come under the control of other brain functions such as memory. We remember sensations that we have felt before, and with the help of these memories we can choose the best way to react to a stimulus. For example, experience tells us that if we see black clouds in the sky it would be sensible to wear something waterproof when we go outside.

Experiences are recorded in the cerebral cortex in memory circuits called *synaptic networks*. These work differently for sensory memory (which stores information for only a few seconds), for short-term memory (which allows us to remember things for a few minutes while we think of them), and for long-term memory (which is virtually limitless).

Memory is linked to many other functions of the brain. Among these is language, the ability to use words to describe both concrete objects and abstract ideas such as emotions or thoughts. In the cerebral cortex there are four centres for language, one each for speaking and writing, and two for understanding these processes. Language allows us to think and convey ideas. Overall, the brain's highest function is probably imagination, the capacity to think and invent.

The higher functions of the brain are dealt with in the front part of the cortex. Again, each has its special area, but these are not duplicated in the left and right hemispheres as are the sensory and motor areas. The left side of the brain is concerned with logical thought, speech and so on; the right side of the brain is more concerned with imagination and artistry.

Each area of the cerebral cortex is specifically linked to a certain part of the body, but the size of these areas bears no relation to the size of the corresponding part of the body. Instead it depends on the numbers of nerves leading from and to them.

Many activities are dealt with only in one hemisphere. In the cortex of the left hemisphere, for example, there are four distinct centres for language.

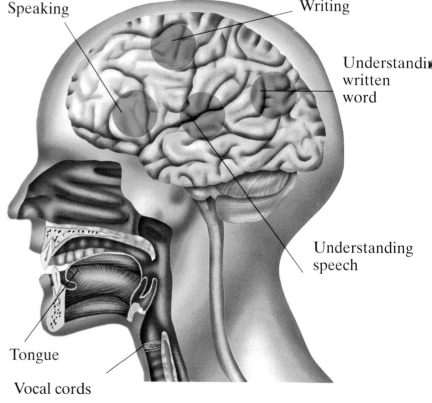

Speaking

Writing

Understandi▶
written
word

Understanding
speech

Tongue

Vocal cords

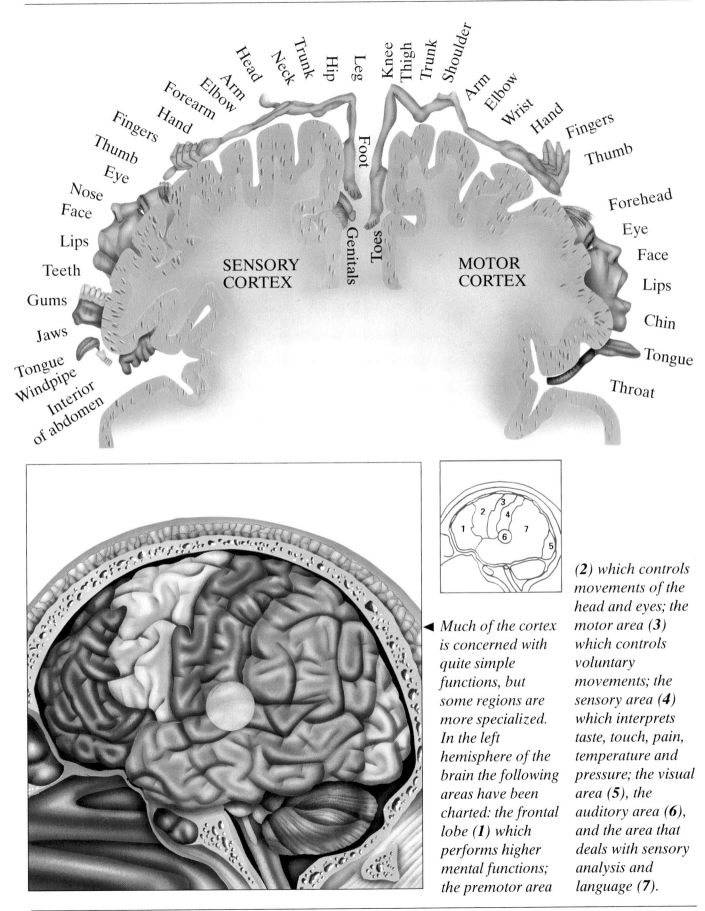

Sensory Cortex labels: Fingers, Thumb, Eye, Nose, Face, Lips, Teeth, Gums, Jaws, Tongue, Windpipe, Interior of abdomen, Forearm, Hand, Arm, Elbow, Head, Neck, Trunk, Hip, Leg, Foot, Genitals, Toes

Motor Cortex labels: Knee, Thigh, Trunk, Shoulder, Arm, Elbow, Wrist, Hand, Fingers, Thumb, Forehead, Eye, Face, Lips, Chin, Tongue, Throat

SENSORY CORTEX

MOTOR CORTEX

◄ *Much of the cortex is concerned with quite simple functions, but some regions are more specialized. In the left hemisphere of the brain the following areas have been charted: the frontal lobe (**1**) which performs higher mental functions; the premotor area (**2**) which controls movements of the head and eyes; the motor area (**3**) which controls voluntary movements; the sensory area (**4**) which interprets taste, touch, pain, temperature and pressure; the visual area (**5**), the auditory area (**6**), and the area that deals with sensory analysis and language (**7**).*

Emotions and sleep

Emotion is the term for a complicated range of feelings – not physical feelings such as pain or heat, but abstract feelings such as sadness or happiness, irritation, jealousy and love. Of course these abstract feelings do have a physical effect: when you are afraid, for example, blood is diverted from your skin to your muscles, so you turn pale. Your muscles contract so that your body is ready to spring into action. This is known as the 'fight or flight' reaction. When you are happy, on the other hand, your body feels relaxed.

Emotion is associated with the *limbic system*, which is located deep inside the brain. This system is connected with other areas of the brain such as the cerebral cortex and the hypothalamus, which are able to control and moderate our emotions to some extent. The limbic system is also concerned with the organization of memory and with appetite, and is closely connected with the brain's smell centres.

Sleep is a necessary time of rest for the body. When we sleep, we lose consciousness, our muscles relax, our body temperature drops a little, and all the internal workings of the body slow down. The heart beats more slowly, blood pressure drops and our breathing also slows down. Sleep is vital to us; if we go without sleep for too long we cannot function efficiently.

When we fall asleep we go through different sleep phases. At first we sleep lightly and the body changes little. Then sleep deepens and the body slows right down.

While we are asleep the brain's activities slow down for part of the time, but about every hour and a half we go through phases when the brain is as active, or even more active, than when we are awake. These periods last between 5 and 20 minutes, and during them we seem to dream more than at other times. Behind closed lids, our eyes move quickly up and down and from side to side, as if we were watching something. These phases are known as REM – rapid eye movement – sleep.

Our sleep pattern seems to be controlled by part of the brain stem called the reticular formation. This is a netlike arrangement of neurons which link together vital centres of the brain. It is also involved in sorting out and selecting which stimuli reach the brain. So many sensations are picked up by our receptors that we cannot possibly think consciously about them all. So the reticular formation makes sure that we are not aware of continuing stimuli which do not need our attention. For example, when it starts to rain we hear the sound of the raindrops falling, but soon we are no longer aware of it. The reticular formation also helps us to keep alert and to concentrate.

The limbic system is closely linked to the corpus callosum (1), the anterior nucleus of the thalamus (2), the olfactory bulb (3), the hypothalamus (4), the amygdaloid bodies (5) and the reticular formation (6). These are all deep inside the brain. Our emotional state

depends on the limbic system, but we have some control over it and our reactions because it is connected to the cerebral cortex.

▼

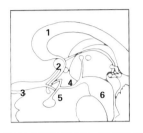

Waking activity

REM sleep

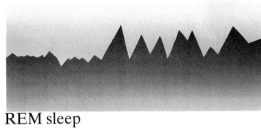

◀ *Cerebral activity is shown by encephalograms, which measure the electrical currents of the brain and show them on a graph. Studying these shows whether there is any alteration in the brain's normal functioning. Encephalograms made when someone is awake (top) and when they are in a phase of REM sleep (below) are fairly similar, showing that during these periods cerebral activity is high.*

Strong emotions such as fear are accompanied by responses of the autonomic nervous system. For example, when you are afraid your hair stands on end, your pupils enlarge, muscles contract and your blood pressure rises. ▼

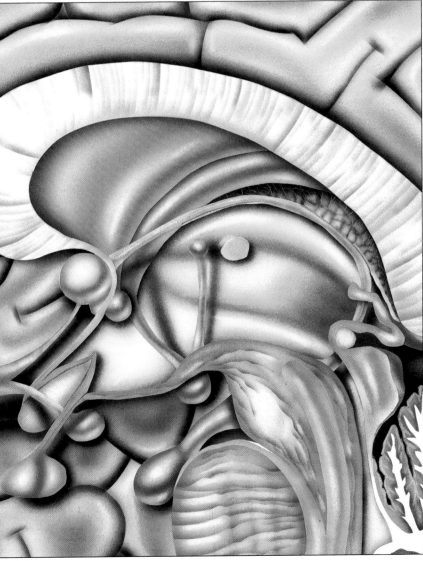

Chest tightens

Heart dilates

Muscles contract

Bladder control weakens

Capillaries constrict

Pupils dilate

Lungs dilate

Blood pressure rises

Adrenalin flows

Hair stands on end

Finding out

Moving without thinking

Many reflex actions are the body's way of removing itself from a source of pain, such as something burning or pricking it. Here is a way of seeing a reflex action without hurting yourself! Take a small hammer and gently tap different parts of your knee. You will find that when you tap it in a certain place, your lower leg will lift up unexpectedly. This is because the stimulus caused by the blow travels to the spinal cord and across to the motor nerve by a reflex arc. Because this circuit has no connection with the brain, you cannot do anything to prevent the knee jerk.

The body's alarm system

The sensation of pain is not simply something tiresome and inconvenient; it is a vital alarm signal which we must take notice of if our bodies are to remain healthy and function properly. Pain is the body's way of telling us that something is being damaged, or is not working correctly, and that we should do something about it. For example, if you spend too long in the sun, your skin starts to feel painful; this warning tells you to get out of the sun as soon as possible because you are at risk of sunburn. Of course, it would have been better to leave before the pain!

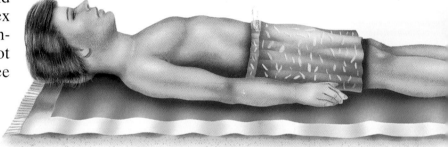

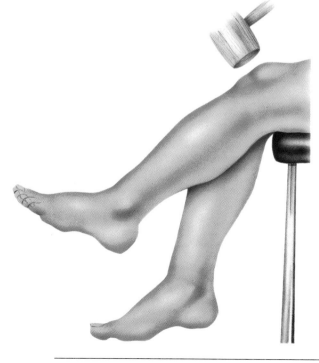

Sweet

Salt

Same question, different answers ...

We all have the same nervous structures, but we do not all respond to sensations in the same way. Some people enjoy sounds that others find unpleasant or even painful, and some people enjoy tastes that others think nasty. Choose four types of food (savoury, sweet, sour and bitter), some strongly scented substances, and some different colours. Then ask your friends to say which they like and which they dislike. You will find that their answers will be different from one another.

Getting used to sensations

As we know, our bodies soon get used to some stimuli. Here is an experiment which shows this very clearly. Fill three containers with water – one hot (but not too hot), one at room temperature and one cooled down with ice cubes. Put one hand into the hot water, and the other into the cold water. At first you will notice the water temperatures, but after a few minutes you will have become used to them and will hardly be aware of them. Now put both hands into the water at room temperature. What sensation do you feel in each hand at first, and after a few minutes? It takes the receptors a little while to adapt to a stimulus.

Hot water

Cold water

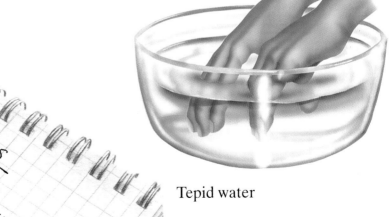

Tepid water

Sour

Bitter

Index and glossary